ROOTS IN TRADITION AND FAMILY

Study by Phill Nall
Commentary by Cecil Sherman

Free downloadable Teaching Guide for this study available at
NextSunday.com/teachingguides

NextSunday Resources
6316 Peake Road
Macon, Georgia 31210-3960
1-800-747-3016
©2019 by NextSunday Resources
All rights reserved.

All Scripture quotations are from the New Revised Standard Version of the
Bible copyright © 1989 by the Division of Christian Education of the National Council of
Churches of Christ in the USA.

TABLE OF CONTENTS

Roots in Tradition and Family

Study Introduction 1

Lesson 1 Tradition
     Luke 2:21-40
     Study 3
     Commentary 11

Lesson 2 Looking for Love in All the Right Places
     Luke 2:41-52
     Study 19
     Commentary 27

Lesson 3 May I Introduce You to a Friend?
     Luke 3:15-22
     Study 35
     Commentary 43

Lesson 4 Home is Where the Heart Is
     Luke 4:14-30
     Study 51
     Commentary 61

How to Use This Study

NextSunday Resources Adult Bible Studies are designed to help adults study Scripture seriously within the context of the larger Christian tradition and, through that process, find their faith renewed, challenged, and strengthened. We study the Scriptures because we believe they affect our current lives in important ways. Each study contains the following three components:

Study Guide

Each study guide lesson is arranged in four movements:

Remembering provides a frame of reference for the Scriptures.

Studying is centered on giving the biblical material in-depth attention while often surrounding it with helpful insights from theology, ethics, church history, and other areas.

Understanding helps us find relevant connections between our lives and the biblical message.

What About Me? provides brief statements that help unite life issues with the meaning of the biblical text.

Commentary

Each study guide lesson is accompanied by an additional, in-depth commentary on the biblical material. Written by a different author than the study guide, each commentary gives the opportunity for learners to approach the Scripture text from a separate but complementary viewpoint.

Teaching Guide

In addition to the provided study guide and commentary, *NextSunday Resources* also provides a *free* downloadable teaching guide, available at NextSunday.com. Each teaching guide gives the teacher tools for focusing on the content of each study guide lesson through additional commentary and Bible background information. Through teacher helps and teaching options, each teaching guide also provides substance for variety and choice in the preparation of each lesson.

Study Introduction

Entering a small conference room, we exchanged suspicious glances and made superficial introductions. It was clear that we all came from various backgrounds, yet our journeys had brought us together—for this one week—in New York City. Taking a moment to survey the room, examine the faces, and really get a sense of each person's presence, I soon discovered that we each had our own story to tell. And that is exactly what we did.

Granted, we took plenty of time out to draw, to color, and to get our stories out into the open, but above all else, we *communed*! Within our small group, autobiographies were taking shape, and not just your standard, "run-of-the-mill" autobiographies. On the contrary, these were *spiritual* autobiographies—the stories of our lives, the stories of our faith.

We began by noting signposts, landmarks, or just any essential events from our lives that we could recall. Then, as we plunged further into our examination, we began taking into consideration the different elements connecting those events. Before long, we all realized just what it was that had held us—*all* of us—together during our most difficult times. Although each of us had experienced very different circumstances, we understood that, in the end, we all relied upon a common denominator: the fact that our hope was rooted in faith.

Over the course of this study, we will be taking a glimpse into a tiny window of Jesus' spiritual autobiography. We will study the early signposts that became the foundation for his spiritual journey, pointing out landmarks that clearly gave him a sense of direction. In this way, we can use any clues we find to discern just what it took for Christ to become fully empowered to fulfill God's mission and purpose.

One thing we all have in common is that each of us has our own history. Some choose to ignore it, while others absorb it. Jesus not only claimed his history, but he even thrived on it, allowing the roots and tradition of Judaism to affect his *whole* life. If we allow them to, our own histories are just as apt to affect us as well and in fact, can even come to dictate our decision-making processes. As you move through this study, write your own spiritual autobiography, discovering for yourself the importance of roots, tradition, and family.

Lesson  Study

TRADITION
Luke 2:21-40

Central Question
How can our faith traditions enhance our understanding of God?

Scripture

Luke 2:21-40 After eight days had passed, it was time to circumcise the child; and he was called Jesus, the name given by the angel before he was conceived in the womb. 22 When the time came for their purification according to the law of Moses, they brought him up to Jerusalem to present him to the Lord 23 (as it is written in the law of the Lord, "Every firstborn male shall be designated as holy to the Lord"), 24 and they offered a sacrifice according to what is stated in the law of the Lord, "a pair of turtledoves or two young pigeons." 25 Now there was a man in Jerusalem whose name was Simeon; this man was righteous and devout, looking forward to the consolation of Israel, and the Holy Spirit rested on him. 26 It had been revealed to him by the Holy Spirit that he would not see death before he had seen the Lord's Messiah. 27 Guided by the Spirit, Simeon came into the temple; and when the parents brought in the child Jesus, to do for him what was customary under the law, 28 Simeon took him in his arms and praised God, saying, 29 "Master, now you are dismissing your servant in peace, according to your word; 30 for my eyes have seen your salvation, 31 which you have prepared in the presence of all peoples, 32 a light for revelation to the Gentiles and for glory to your people Israel." 33 And the child's father and mother were amazed at what was being said about him. 34 Then Simeon blessed them and said to his mother Mary, "This child is destined for the falling and the rising of many in Israel, and to be a sign that will be opposed 35 so that the inner thoughts of many will be revealed—and a sword will pierce your own soul too." 36 There was also a prophet, Anna the daughter of Phanuel, of the tribe of Asher. She was of a great age, having lived with her husband seven years after her marriage, 37 then as a widow to the age of eighty-four. She never left the temple but worshiped there with fasting and prayer night and day. 38 At that moment she came, and began to praise God and to speak about the child to all who were looking for the redemption of Jerusalem. 39 When they had finished everything required by the law of the Lord, they returned to Galilee, to their own town of Nazareth. 40 The child grew and became strong, filled with wisdom; and the favor of God was upon him.

Remembering

Bethlehem—just the word brings to mind memories of manger scenes, church Christmas pageants, and carols sung around the piano. Located in the heart of Palestine, just south of Jerusalem, this small town is where our story begins. Although surrounded by barren land, Bethlehem itself actually is a rather fertile region, full of everything from fig and olive trees to sheep and wheat fields. Interestingly enough, in Hebrew, "Bethlehem" literally means "the house of bread." In light of this, how appropriate that the "Bread of Life" would be born there!

As his parents wanted to preserve the customs of his people, Jesus was circumcised and named on the eight day after his birth. In Palestine, names were used for descriptive purposes. They could refer to circumstances surrounding the birth (for instance, Jacob, meaning "trickster"), or they might even refer to a specific physical characteristic of the newborn (like Laban, meaning "white" or "blond"). Then again, a child could also receive the name of a parent, suggesting some aspect of either that parent's personality or convictions (for example, Saul, meaning "asked for," or Elijah, "Jehovah is my God"). Mary and Joseph, on the other hand, did not have to choose a name; they had been given one. The angel had already told Mary, "You shall call him Jesus." Obediently, the couple followed this divine instruction and named their child Jesus—or in Hebrew, Joshua, meaning "He will save."

In this lesson, our story moves from Bethlehem to Jerusalem. In keeping with the traditions of the day, Joseph and Mary journey with their son to the Holy City to participate in the ritual of purification—in other words, to present the child to the Lord. While there, Joseph and Mary encounter two prophets who reconfirm that Jesus' life indeed will be special. Then, almost as a news report would offer a brief aside, Luke tells us that when the trio returned home, Jesus grew in wisdom and strength, affirming that God was truly with him. But what we hear as merely a simple, matter-of-fact conclusion to the narrative, we know is truly the setting in motion of a miracle.

Studying

It was in following the traditions of the Jewish faith that Joseph and Mary encountered the prophetic couple in the Jerusalem Temple. While we never want to enslave ourselves to tradition, it can nevertheless be a powerful means of connecting the future with what is meaningful from our past. Five times in this chapter, Luke tells us that Joseph and Mary closely followed the traditions of the law. For starters, Jesus was circumcised on the eighth day (2:21), after which Mary went on to observe the practice of purification (2:22-24). Next, as tradition dictated every year, Jesus' parents went to the Passover feast in Jerusalem (2:41). Of course, Jesus' trip to Jerusalem also was a traditional rite of dedication (2:42), and finally, we see him portrayed as a child who obeys the commandments (2:51). This information is particularly significant to us because it highlights the righteous upbringing Jesus' parents offered him. In addition, it also means that Jesus later will be able to speak to religious leaders as an insider, as one raised in the very same system he will come to critique.

Obedience to the Law (2:21-24) In accordance with Levitical law (Lev 12:3), Joseph and Mary have Jesus circumcised on the eighth day after his birth. Not regarded as a mere physical act, circumcision symbolized the covenant relationship between God and the Hebrew people. Earlier in ancient Israel's history, the naming of the child took place immediately upon birth; however, as the value and importance of circumcision increased, the naming also came to be reserved for the eighth day. These rituals were established as a means of connecting people with both God and the entire community of faith.

In Luke's Gospel, the inclusion of the purification ceremony emphasizes not only the righteousness of Mary, a Jewish woman following her tradition, but also Jesus' first visit to the Temple in Jerusalem. The ceremony itself took place 40 days after birth in the case of a male child, 80 days afterward in the case of a female child. Until the ceremony was carried out, the new mother was considered "unclean," and therefore, was forbidden to touch anything sacred or even to enter the Temple itself (Lev 12:1-8). Since only the woman was considered unclean and in need of purification, scribes from the ancient world along with modern biblical commentators have puzzled over Luke's language in this text pointing to "their" purification. However, given his concern in showing that the family closely followed tradition, Luke is probably speaking loosely of this trip to the Temple as being a "family matter."

> According to Jewish tradition, a mother's being labeled "unclean" after childbirth had nothing to do with physical cleanliness. Rather, it was considered a spiritual issue.

The act of dedicating Jesus to God may have some traditional background as well. However, some scholars point out that we have no real evidence that this kind of dedication was actually practiced. Yet, these studies have too quickly overlooked texts like Nehemiah 10:35-36, in which the people of ancient Israel commit themselves to offer to God their firstborn sons, as is written in the law (Ex 22:29). For Luke, Jesus' dedication was neither unusual nor unique, but instead, a common

> You shall not delay to make offerings from the fullness of your harvest and from the outflow of your presses. The firstborn of your sons you shall give to me. (Ex 22:29)

practice among pious parents. The process surrounding this event followed the outline prescribed in Leviticus 12:8. In other words, the sacrifice was intended for *Mary*, not Jesus. In the meantime, it is also noteworthy that the use of doves was a special consideration given to the poor and to travelers, since livestock were both expensive and difficult to move over long distances.

The Practice of Faith (2:25-38) Make no mistake—by following their traditions Mary and Joseph were not merely fulfilling obligations; they were *practicing* their faith. Their conscientiousness and piety resulted in a meeting that yet again confirmed their beliefs about their child. But, then again, perhaps this is not too terribly surprising, especially since faith often puts us in places where God can affirm our efforts.

As we continue on in our text, we find that Mary and Joseph reap the benefits of two independent and prophetic testimonies concerning Jesus' identity. The first testimony comes from Simeon, a "devout" man "full of the Holy Spirit." By the Spirit, Simeon learns that he will not die before he sees the Messiah, and by that same Spirit, the prophet is guided to the Temple where he meets Jesus' family. Simeon praises God for this most blessed gift and assists the family in dedicating Jesus to God.

> Simeon's words compose a hymn, referred to since the fourth century as the *Nunc Dimittis*, which means, "Now let thou depart." The hymn praises the far-reaching implications of Jesus' incarnation—that is, his coming to earth in human form. Unlike the hymn offered by the angels at Jesus' birth (2:14), this one includes the welfare not only of ancient Israel but of the Gentiles as well (2:32). Upon first glance, Simeon immediately recognizes in Jesus the promised one of salvation.

After blessing the couple, Simeon focuses his attention solely on Mary. The old man's words, however, are ominous. Foreshadowing what Jesus will say about himself (12:51-53), the aged prophet reveals that Jesus will cause division in ancient Israel, indicating that there must first be a "fall" before there is a "rise," clearly a reference to Jesus' death and Resurrection. In a way, this message prepares Mary for the overwhelming pain that will come when her son is crucified on a cross (2:35b).

Notice that, as is typical of Luke's writing, he pairs together a male and a female. Although Simeon announces to the couple what will yet be, Anna is the one described as a "prophetess." Anna's age, her status as a widow, and her piety in worship "day and night" (Acts 26:7) are all intended to show the depth of her relationship with God. As prophetess, her role in this account is to proclaim the good news of Jesus to the people. She serves as a herald, a preacher of God's salvation to all who will listen. Anna's proclamation concludes the events in the Temple, but she—along with Simeon and Jesus' parents—reminds us that those who are genuinely dedicated to God are able to recognize God's work in the world.

> Zechariah and Elizabeth, Mary and Joseph, and now Simeon and Anna are only 3 of 13 male/female pairs noted throughout Luke (see 4:25-27; 7:36-50; 15:3-10).

A Traditional Family? (2:39-40) As mentioned earlier, Luke informs us that this family of piety returns home after these spectacular events to "business as usual." Yet, those who are familiar with the story know better. At home, Jesus grows in wisdom and stature, and once again, Luke reminds us that all things necessary under the law are fulfilled. Jesus will begin his ministry as an insider, raised in a traditional and religious home of faithful parents.

The beginning verses of this lesson's passage (21-24) along with these last two verses (39-40) "sandwich" Jesus' early life, fulfilling Luke's need to assure his readers that the Messiah was raised in a home steeped with tradition. Luke reinforces this aspect of Jesus' early years not only for tradition's sake, but to point out that this era in the Messiah's life eventually will speak to his ability to understand all factions of the religious system—both good and bad. Noting that the "grace of God was upon him," the Gospel writer stresses God's presence in Jesus' life even as a child. Clearly, the truth of this statement is most blatant because Jesus is the Son of God. Yet, at the same time, it is true because Jesus reaped the benefits of what his parents had sown into his life at a very early age.

Understanding

These days, the word "traditional" is often considered a bad one, referring to anything outdated, overused, boring, and sentimental. For example, many churches are presently facing issues pushing them to choose between what has been deemed contemporary and the "traditional" way of doing ministry. Meanwhile, families have found value in establishing traditions, whether they coincide with mealtimes, holidays, bedtime routines, or even annual trips. Likewise, many schools also observe long-standing traditions that have proven significant for passing on values and commitment.

So, what exactly can we learn from tradition? For the earthly parents of Jesus, tradition provided an avenue for expressing their devotion to God. Within their religious traditions, the couple was able to engrain into Jesus' mind the importance of being devoted to God. Remember, God *chose* Mary and Joseph as Jesus' parents, and we would do well not to underestimate their role in training him. On one level, Mary and Joseph's religious practice provided a means for teaching Jesus about the faith of his ancestors. On another level, though, their traditions also assured them of God's blessing and presence in the raising of Jesus. Raising God's child—what a daunting, yet awe-inspiring and privileged challenge!

Simon's and Anna's blessings reminded Jesus' parents of the enormous ramifications of the task that lay before them. Within our own churches, our role is no different, in that we also are to advocate for children even as we commit ourselves to their upbringing. Like the prophet and prophetess from this lesson's account, we are called to alert the parents of today that they have in their care some very special children of God, ministers already called by God to participate in the advent of the Kingdom.

What About Me?

- *Learn from your traditions.* Traditions are valuable teaching tools that help us connect our past with our future. However, we should never be guilty of enslaving ourselves to practicing our faith in the same way. In every tradition, there is room for creativity of expression. Seek ways to enrich the religious traditions of your faith in worship, education, and ministry.

- *Practice your faith tangibly.* Mary and Joseph lived out what they believed, even "going the extra mile" to keep their faith commitments. Too easily and too often we allow what we think is important to overshadow what is ultimate: the daily living of our faith.

- *Pass it on.* The church need never forget its responsibility to its children. Jesus was raised by faithful parents who instilled in him the basic tenants of the Hebrew faith. They helped lay the foundation for what he was to become. Our responsibility to our own children can be no less deliberate.

Resources

William Barclay, *The Gospel of Luke* (Philadelphia: The Westminster Press, 1975).

Charles R. Erdman, *The Gospel of Luke* (Philadelphia: The Westminster Press, 1949).

S. MacLean Gilmour, "Luke," *The Interpreter's Bible*, vol. 8 (New York: Abingdon Press, 1952).

Rabbi H. Kushner, quoted by P. Berman, *The Courage of Conviction* (New York: Ballantine, 1985) 164.

TRADITION
Luke 2:21-40

Introduction

Quite possibly, you are all too familiar with the pattern: One night you are minding your own business, reading the paper, doing a little work after hours or just watching television, when suddenly the phone rings. In our case, it was our daughter calling. At first the conversation followed its normal routine, but soon there came a pause. "Mother, Dad—we're going to have a baby." And immediately, we came alive! "When is this going to be? Are you well? How do you feel? Are you comfortable with your doctor?" And on and on our animated questions flowed, one into the next. Needless to say, it was big news, and with our daughter's blessing, we began to tell anyone and everyone who would stand still long enough to hear.

Months passed before the big day. There were a few tense times, but overall things went well. Then, in April of 1987, we got the news. Genie was in labor. A few anxious hours later, our son-in-law Doug called with a report. It was a healthy, eight-pound boy. His name was Nathaniel (meaning "gift of God"). And best of all, Mother was doing well. My wife, on the other hand, was not about to stand around in Fort Worth, Texas, while her daughter was adjusting to being a new mother several states away in Madison, Wisconsin. In fact, as soon as Genie arrived home from the hospital, Dot was waiting for her in Madison. I drove up a few days later. And, of course, there was another set of grandparents who lived in Nederland, Texas. They too had traveled to Wisconsin. More than pleased—not to mention, thankful for such a blessing—all stood with wonder, awe, and admiration before the beautiful infant.

Nathaniel was the first grandchild in our family on either side. In fact, to this day he remains my and Dot's only grandchild. Even from the day Genie announced his impending birth, Nathaniel was eagerly, anxiously awaited. The precious event of our first grandchild's entering the world brought both sets of grandparents to Madison. And naturally, gifts were showered, heaped, lavished upon the baby. Our words of adoration and gratitude to God seemed too few to suffice in light of such a gift. So, what then, you ask? Well, to make a long story short, all went back to normal—that is, for everyone except Genie and Doug. They were new parents, and life would never be the same for them again. While *we* merely went home, *they* went to work as parents.

Now, the question remains, why tell this story at all? Quite simply, it serves as a perfect introduction to our text. Jesus also was born amid a fanfare that exceeded anything his family had ever encountered. But, when all the hoopla was said and done, Mary and Joseph were still left with a baby boy and the task of being parents.

With Simeon and Anna's proclamations, this lesson's text maintains a hint of the fanfare from Jesus' birth, but what emerges is the beginning of a pattern and tradition of Jewish child rearing. Often we make too much of the fanfare and too little of the godly pattern. Although none of our children is likely to be recognized as a future prophet, all of our children need godly pattern.

Fanfare to Pattern, 2:21-24.

The birth of Jesus was accompanied by several singular acts of God, acts that were unusual, unlikely, and by all means, miraculous. Zechariah and Elizabeth, for instance, were too old to have a baby, yet they did. His name was John, and he would not only to go before Jesus but even baptize him at the onset of his earthly ministry. Meanwhile, an exceptional young woman named Mary would consent to carry this child, Jesus. Then who can forget Joseph, the man of great faith who agreed to maintain his engagement to Mary even though he knew people would cast a suspicious eye on their situation? And, of course, later on shepherds who were keeping their flocks near Bethlehem encountered an angel of God who announced to them the birth of Jesus. Now, here's some fanfare. After all, not only did the shepherds rush to adore and wonder at the newborn, but wise men also came from the East to bring gifts and to lift up their thanks to God for the child. Admittedly, the birth of *any* child is a signal event for a family, but the birth of Jesus was attended by the spectacular.

And then it was over. Mary and Joseph were left with a child, but they also had a sort of parenting manual to go by, for Judaism took any new child of the faith very seriously. William Barclay dipped into both Greek thought and Jewish pattern when he said, "A child is a gift of God. The Stoics used to say that a child was not given a parent, but only lent. Of all God's gifts there is none for which we shall be so answerable as the gift of a child" (*The Gospel of Luke*, Philadelphia: Westminster Press, 1956, 25). But more than faith assumptions guided Mary and Joseph, for Jesus grew up in a family that meticulously observed the law of Moses. In fact, no fewer than five times throughout the Scripture passage, Luke insists that Mary and Joseph were consistent in doing *everything* required of them by the law (Fred Craddock, *Luke*, Interpretation, Louisville: John Knox Press, 1990, 38).

Naturally, though, since Jesus grew up to pronounce judgment on institutional Judaism, we are easily inclined to take lightly the great good inherent to the very Judaism that produced him. Circumcision, purification, offerings, official naming—these were the marked paths devout parents followed. Yet, these public acts of obedience to Jewish rule are only suggestions of the private devotions that surrounded Jesus from infancy to adulthood. Jesus was expected to attend not only synagogue every week, but also what was essentially a parochial school of Judaism. In the meantime, his family religiously observed the great feasts in Jerusalem and attended them whenever they could afford it. Without question, Mary was chosen to mother Jesus because she was exceptionally devout (see Lk 1:28). Clearly, that sense of devotion spilled over into other aspects of her life as well.

Even though most readers of this commentary probably are not Jewish, many of you most likely have come from home environments much like the one that produced Jesus. My family went to church every Sunday. This kind of pattern has produced some of the best people I've ever known. Education and life would naturally expand our minds, but by no means could they shake our patterns. I am grateful to be a product of such a system, especially when I realize that Jesus was reared under quite similar circumstances.

Piety and Recognition, 2:25-38.

There are two particular episodes from Jesus' infancy:

(1) As Mary and Joseph were going into the Temple "to do for him what was customary under the law," a man named Simeon "took him (Jesus) in his arms and praised God" (2:28). The Lord had promised him that he would not die until he had seen the long-anticipated Messiah. Upon his first glance at the baby Jesus, Simeon realized through the power of the Holy Spirit that this was indeed the child he had been waiting for. After praising God, the old prophet rejoiced that he was ready to embrace death, renewed with the hope of better things to come as he pronounced Jesus "a light to the Gentiles and a glory to your people Israel" (2:32).

Following this, we as readers gain a sure sign that Simeon was in fact in tune with the Spirit of God. Note that he did not just praise and fawn over the baby Jesus, but he also disclosed a prophetic warning: "This child is destined for the falling and the rising of many in Israel, and to be a sign that will be opposed...a sword will pierce your own soul too" (2:34-35). Mary surely recalled Simeon's words as she stood beneath the cross, as she wept at her dying son's feet, as she wondered what in the world he must have been thinking by challenging the scribes and Pharisees. There was glory for Mary in being the mother of Jesus, to be sure, but there also was enormous pain and sorrow.

(2) As Simeon was praising God and speaking prophetic words about the baby Jesus, the prophet Anna approached Mary, Joseph, and the baby, praising God and speaking about the child "to all

who were looking for the redemption of Jerusalem" (2:28). What are we to make of this detail? Was Jesus unusual in appearance? I don't think so. In fact, he probably was a rather "normal" baby as far as babies go.

The abnormal and the exceptional, however, are found underlying the words of Simeon and Anna. Although the religious system of that day may have been rotten at the top, down where ordinary people lived and practiced devotions there is much worth our imitation. Both Simeon and Anna were looking forward in faith, believing wholeheartedly that God was not yet finished with Israel. The coming of Christ only confirmed their faith. In addition, they practiced their faith, which likely had much to do with their unusual spiritual insight. Besides, we know that prayer, Bible study, and church attendance are merely the basics, whereas authentic spiritual enlightenment comes from patterned holy living. Note the mystics, John Wesley, or even the Puritans; all acknowledged a pattern of holiness that welcomed in spiritual insight. And finally, Simeon and Anna both were able to discern a prophet at first glance, which is far more than most of us can say for ourselves. Why, just consider how few recognized Jesus even when he was performing miracles and speaking with great wisdom. This makes it all the more amazing that Simeon and Anna saw him for who he was, even when he had neither miracles nor parables to his name.

Nazareth, Obscurity, and Parenting, 2:39-40.

"When they had finished everything required by the law of the Lord, they returned to Galilee, to their own town of Nazareth" (2:39). What can we say about Nazareth? Walter Russell Bowie wrote, "In general estimation Nazareth was a place of no consequence; an obscure village off the main highway, in the Galilean hills. In the whole Old Testament it is never mentioned" (*The Compassionate Christ*, New York: Abingdon Press, 1965, 56). Apparently, Joseph and Mary never had any intent whatsoever "to give Jesus every advantage." In other words, he was not reared like he was somebody special. His parents were people of respectable character who led decent lives and maintained an orderly household. In light of this, let's take a look at an excerpt from a guide about child-rearing, written in 1962 by the Archdeacon of Chesterfield in England:

> Begin from infancy to give the child everything he wants. In this way he will grow up to believe that the world owes him a living. Never give him any spiritual training. Wait until he is twenty-one, and then let him decide for himself. Avoid the use of the word "wrong." It may develop a guilt complex. This will condition him to believe later when he is arrested for stealing a car that society is against him and he is being persecuted. Give the child all the spending money he wants. Never let him earn his own. Why should he have things as tough as you had them? Satisfy his every craving for food and drink and comfort. See that every desire is gratified. Denial may lead to harmful frustration. Take his part against neighbors, teachers, and policemen. They are all prejudiced against your child. When he gets into real trouble, apologize for yourself by saying, "I never could do anything with him." Prepare yourself for a life of grief. You will have it. (Ibid., 45)

Silence in the Gospels does not give us a biblical base for what I am saying, but what we know of Jewish pattern does. Jesus was reared to be a hard worker by a family that had very little, but by parents who practiced what they preached. His neighbors were much like his parents, so in a sense he could have been reared by the Nazareth community. And so was I, just as most of you are products of this same pattern. Nowadays, "family and tradition" are not universally popular ideas, but if we intend to turn out good children and grandchildren, I don't know any better way of doing so than by rooting them within the foundation of these two elements. If it was good enough for Jesus, then surely it is good enough for the rest of us.

Notes

Notes

Lesson Study

Looking for Love in All the Right Places
Luke 2:41-52

Central Question
Where do *you* look for Jesus?

Scripture

Luke 2:41-52 Now every year his parents went to Jerusalem for the festival of the Passover. 42 And when he was twelve years old, they went up as usual for the festival. 43 When the festival was ended and they started to return, the boy Jesus stayed behind in Jerusalem, but his parents did not know it. 44 Assuming that he was in the group of travelers, they went a day's journey. Then they started to look for him among their relatives and friends. 45 When they did not find him, they returned to Jerusalem to search for him. 46 After three days they found him in the temple, sitting among the teachers, listening to them and asking them questions. 47 And all who heard him were amazed at his understanding and his answers. 48 When his parents saw him they were astonished; and his mother said to him, "Child, why have you treated us like this? Look, your father and I have been searching for you in great anxiety." 49 He said to them, "Why were you searching for me? Did you not know that I must be in my Father's house?" 50 But they did not understand what he said to them. 51 Then he went down with them and came to Nazareth, and was obedient to them. His mother treasured all these things in her heart. 52 And Jesus increased in wisdom and in years, and in divine and human favor.

Remembering

When we left our story, Mary and Joseph had just circumcised and named their child. As the firstborn male in their family, Jesus was considered by Mary and Joseph's culture to be sacred to God. Forty days after the birth of a male child, a woman could enter the Temple and participate in a religious ceremony of purification. During the ceremony, the woman was to provide a lamb for a burnt offering and a young pigeon for a sin offering. If she happened to be poor, and therefore unable to bring a lamb, another pigeon could be substituted. This is exactly what Mary did.

As we pick up where we last left off in the Scripture, we learn that this was not the first time Jesus and his parents visited the Temple. Emphasizing yet again that Jesus' parents were people of deep spiritual piety, Luke records that it was their yearly custom to travel to Jerusalem for the feast of the Passover, one of the most important events observed in Judaism.

> In addition to the ancient rituals of circumcision and purification, a firstborn son also underwent the ceremony called the Redemption of the Firstborn (Num 18:16). During this ceremony, the parents, in a sense, could "buy back" their son from God, a privilege that required the payment of five shekels to the priests. However, we have no indication that Mary and Joseph paid the money to "buy back" Jesus (Barclay, 24).

Just after Passover, Jesus left his parents and found his way into the Temple. There he sat among religious teachers and priests, listening and questioning. As they watched this child captivate an entire audience, the adults were amazed at the depth of Jesus' understanding. When his parents finally found him—three whole days later—they were understandably upset. For 12 years they had loved, taught, and cared for him as best they could. And although God had confirmed and reconfirmed Jesus' identity and mission, their child's words to them must have come as quite a shock: "I must be in my Father's house." But, after all, we know that Jesus indeed is more than "their" child. In fact, he is more than just "a" child. He is *the* Child of God, Savior, Messiah. God's gift to the world came in the blessed package of

Jesus, who grew under the tutelage of pious parents and a community that took its faith seriously.

Studying

The passage assigned for this session is the only biblical record we have of Jesus' childhood. "It has been said that the boyhood of Jesus is like a walled garden from which we have been given a single flower, but this is so fragrant as to fill our hearts with a longing to enter within the secret enclosure" (Erdman, 36-7). Jesus grew up not only among other Jews, but also in a Jewish home. In his community, education was very important. In school, boys learned their prayers along with the texts of the Torah. They often would recite, "Torah Tzivah Lanu Moshe Morashah Kehilat Ya'akov," or "The Torah which Moses taught us is the inheritance of the Jewish people." In fact, students learned Hebrew, the language of the Torah, although many of them spoke Aramaic at home (Pessin, 110).

Learning was not confined to the schools, however. For instance, it was common for children to learn not only the prayers and customs of their people at home, but also the trades of their parents. In other words, typically a farmer's child would learn to plow and till the soil, whereas a shepherd's child would learn to tend the flocks. Similarly, a carpenter's child might naturally be expected to learn how to work with wood.

> In the year 60 BC, Simeon ben Shetah, a Pharisee leader in the Sanhedrin, made it compulsory for communities to provide education for children who had no fathers to teach them. Later, High Priest Joshua ben Gamala had a law passed stating that every community populated with at least ten families must have a school (Pessin, 110).

As all young people do, the children of Jesus' day learned by watching and asking questions. For instance, when they inquired into why corners of the field were not harvested, someone would explain to them that the grain was left there for the poor. This practice helped teach the children to care for those in need. Likewise, when they asked why the field was not plowed during the seventh year, they were told that all things—even the fields—needed rest. This illustrated for the children the importance of keeping the Sabbath. And, of course, traveling was always good for stirring up useful teaching moments, in that it gave parents an opportunity to point out important landmarks of their faith to curious "followers-to-be."

The Journey to Jerusalem (2:41-42) Although we are told that Mary and Joseph traveled to Jerusalem each year to observe the Feast of Passover, the Scripture does not disclose whether Jesus ever joined them before this trip at the age of 12. On the other hand, we do know that two routes led to Jerusalem from Nazareth, one through Jericho and one through Samaria, each approximately 70 miles long. On foot, it was a four- to five-day journey, and since sojourners had to depend on the hospitality of others along the way, we can easily see why travel was so difficult in those days. Then again, either alternative would have made for an excellent opportunity to share significant moments from Jewish history.

Jesus in Jerusalem—Alone (2:43-6) Following the seven days of Passover festivities, families traveled in groups back to their homelands. The women and children usually got a head start and the men would catch up by nightfall. Jesus' family moved closer and closer to Nazareth, but although Mary and Joseph did not yet realize it, Jesus was not with them. Each parent probably assuming that the other had Jesus under their wing, they traveled a whole day's journey without the boy!

By nightfall, it became apparent that Jesus was nowhere to be found. One can only imagine the countless questions the couple was asked as they started their

> Little is known about the early life of Jesus, perhaps because the early church seems to have had no interest in recording Christ's life until he emerged as a teacher. "At a later date unfettered imagination undertook to make up the deficiency. Compilations of legends such as the Gospel of Thomas gave marvelous and often grotesque and repulsive accounts of Jesus as an exhibitionist and as a boy wonder. The simplicity and restraint of Luke's story stand out in contrast" (Gilmour, 66).

pursuit among relatives: "When was the last time you saw him?" "Whom was he with?" "Where was he?" Yet, coming up empty, they returned to Jerusalem, frantic with worry over what measures to take next. Luke tells us that it wasn't until three days later that they found Jesus in the Temple, "sitting among the teachers, listening to them and asking them questions." Don't make the mistake of overlooking the significance of the

number of days Jesus was missing. For *three days* his parents thought the worst. For *three days* they believed their hopes and dreams for their son might be over. So similar was their situation to what Mary and the disciples would go through some 21 years later, that we cannot help but regard this incident as a foreshadowing of what was yet to come.

The Response (2:47-49) This section of the passage is reminiscent of the response to Jesus' birth in 2:18: "And all who heard it were amazed." What a testimony for Mary and Joseph to hear about their child! Besides, parents can fill a child's head with facts, but for the child actually to understand and connect those facts with real life and then be able to communicate that understanding to others—now, *that* is quite an achievement!

Upon entering the Temple and discovering Jesus there, Mary and Joseph were astonished. Just imagine the looks on their faces and the thoughts running through their heads in that instant! Even as they made their way over to Jesus, Mary scolded, "Child, why have you treated us like this? Look, your father and I have been searching for you in great anxiety." Jesus was already 12 years old, and according to tradition he had become a man, a son of the law, yet Mary still referred to him as a "child." Clearly, in his mother's mind, Jesus' actions were indeed childlike.

Many insist that Jesus' response to his parents was harsh, but closer examination of the text reveals his underlying intent: "Did you not know that I must be in my Father's house?" Jesus realized who he was, and therefore, his parents had to as well—just as we modern Christians are expected to do in our own day and time. These first words ever attributed to Jesus could not be more appropriate! How many spend every day of their lives searching frantically for Jesus? Yet, his very first words cry out to these same seekers: "Why were you searching for me? Did you not know that I must be in my Father's house?"

At Home (2:50-52) Surely, Mary and Joseph must have struggled with the implications of Jesus' words to them. But because he was ever an obedient child, Jesus went home with the couple to Nazareth and "increased in wisdom and in years, and in divine and human favor."

Understanding

Family reunions offer us a chance to connect—or *reconnect*—with our past. Most often at these functions, we hear the stories that have been passed down from one generation to the next and in turn will be passed on to those in the future. To put it plainly, these accounts are the ones you can expect to hear repeatedly throughout your lifetime.

Jesus' trip to Jerusalem resembled a family reunion, in that he heard along the way those stories that linked the families of the past to the families of the present. Why, he probably even played with cousins, and maybe even got his cheeks pinched by that one aunt whose tag line always seems to be, "Jesus, you are getting more handsome every day." But imagine, in the middle of all the festivities, a child goes missing, and without hesitation, an entire family responds.

Mary and Joseph's search for Jesus should speak to each of us. When we set out to look for Jesus, where do we start? With relatives and friends? The world? Success? Our jobs? How long does it take us to hear Jesus' question, "Why were you searching for me?" Can we honestly say that we even understand what he means? But perhaps the first question we should ask ourselves is, why would we even attempt to look for Jesus today in the first place? His parents' search we can understand. Yet, perfectly self-reliant people still feel compelled to seek Jesus—and for too many reasons to count. To find him, we must first follow in his parents' footsteps: We must seek diligently. We must look in all the obvious places. And once found, we must cling to him.

What About Me?

- *Traditions are important, but don't lose Jesus in the process.* The possibility is very real that we can follow routine to the point that meaning becomes lost or beauty destroyed. As a prime example, in our worship we can just go through the motions without ever realizing that Jesus is not present.

- *Look for love in the right places.* Remember and treasure past experiences when you were certain of Jesus' presence. Then, during those times when you feel alone, revisit those places where you have met him before.

- *Increase in divine and human favor.* Human favor is given such high priority in our culture that we too often forget God's desire for us to grow in divine favor as well. How would you evaluate your commitment to growing in divine favor?

- *Assist others in their own search for Jesus.* There are many who have yet to discover Jesus' love. Be deliberate in helping others find the pathway to Christ.

Resources

William Barclay, *The Gospel of Luke* (Philadelphia: The Westminster Press, 1975).

Charles R. Erdman, *The Gospel of Luke* (Philadelphia: The Westminster Press, 1949).

S. MacLean Gilmour, "Luke," *The Interpreter's Bible*, vol. 8 (New York: Abingdon Press, 1952).

Madeleine L'Engle, *The Glorious Impossible* (New York: Simon and Schuster, 1990).

Looking for Love in All the Right Places
Luke 2:41-52

Introduction

The time spanning the birth accounts of Jesus to his baptism was 30 years. In fact, those years are silent in the Gospels—silent, that is, except for in this lesson's Scripture passage. Clearly, Luke was a careful biographer. This is clear not just because it is my opinion, but because Luke says so himself: "I decided, after investigating everything carefully from the very first, to write an orderly account for you" (Lk 1:3). Actually, Luke was the writer; but some suggest that Mary is our source.

When Jesus was just 12 years old, something happened that Mary could not ever forget. Hers is a story that most parents share, at least in some form or another. There is a window into the mind of the child, and that window reveals more in retrospect than the parents are able to recognize in the moment. This lesson's text relates such an instance. In hindsight, we understand that the episode really was a clue, a pointer to the person Jesus was becoming. The passage may be short and the story simple, but there is more to it than you might initially expect.

A Son of the Law: Judaism and Tradition, 2:41-43, 46-47.

"Now every year his parents went to Jerusalem for the festival of the Passover. And when he was twelve years old, they went up as usual for the festival" (2:41-42). As in the last session, here again Luke makes it plain that Jesus was reared in the context of strict, devout Judaism, and Jewish law commanded that every male Jew who lived within 15 miles of Jerusalem must attend the Passover (William Barclay, *The Gospel of Luke*, Philadelphia: Westminster Press, 1956, 29). Although Nazareth was much further from

Jerusalem than 15 miles, Mary and Joseph made the effort nevertheless. Passover lasted a week, and the journey was hard. That they went every year only underlines just how enduring their home was under the Jewish faith. Since he would have been considered a child until the age of 12, this trip to Passover was probably the first Jesus had ever made. At 12, he had his bar mitzvah, and as a "son of the law," was under obligation to go to Passover.

Nazareth was a backwater, so certainly the trip to Jerusalem had to be exciting. After all, it was a sure sign to Jesus that he was growing up. Temple ritual and sacrifice, huge crowds and city life—all would have been both delightful and awesome to the 12-year-old. In fact, it apparently was almost *too* exciting, for when the time came to go back to Nazareth, Jesus stayed behind. For the record, I don't necessarily think Mary and Joseph were careless parents. Consider, a sizeable number of their relatives and friends made the trip to Jerusalem with them (see 2:44). They looked out for each other as all the kids ran together. Besides, I imagine the children wanted to be separated from the adults then just as they do nowadays. Joseph and Mary went a full day's journey before noticing that Jesus was missing. Assuming that he was with some other part of their group, they waited in hopes that he would soon show up.

By nightfall, it became obvious that Jesus was nowhere to be found. Immediately, Mary and Joseph returned to the city to find their son, and after three long days of anxious searching, they finally found him. He was "in the temple sitting among the teachers of the law, listening to them and asking them questions. And all who heard him were amazed at his understanding and his answers" (2:46-47).

(1) Jesus gave Mary and Joseph some real pain. Three days of looking for one's son in a big city is no joke. Jesus was doing something very good by putting himself in the company of "the teachers" (2:46), but being a good "son of the law" made him a difficult son for Mary and Joseph.
(2) In reference to this particular Scripture, religious art has made Jesus out to be a precocious child instructing his seniors.

While this may make for good art, it is nevertheless poor interpretation. At Passover, the wisest teachers of the law made themselves available to pilgrims, and Jesus was only taking advantage of this opportunity. "Jesus sits in the temple among the teachers as a child of unusual understanding" (Fred Craddock, *Luke*, Interpretation, Louisville: John Knox Press, 1990, 42). Note, Luke is not telling us that Jesus was teaching the wise men. On the contrary, all we are told is that Jesus was unusual in his interest for and understanding of the law—even at the tender age of 12.

(3) By the time Jesus was full-grown, he was accomplished in the law of Moses and the religion of the Jews, having come to this full understanding by family and study. When Jesus argued with Pharisees, he was not overmatched, but was drawing on a tradition that made him fully Jewish in the very best sense. And when he spoke judgment against Judaism, he spoke from *within* the system as a "son of the law."

A Son of Mary and Joseph: Tension and Obedience, 2:48-51.

"Child, why have you treated us like this? Look, your father and I have been searching for you in great anxiety" (2:48a). If this verse were paraphrased using modern "street language," it might sound something like this: "Kid, for three days we've looked all over this town for you. We've been scared stiff that something bad had happened to you. Where is your mind?" There is no denying that we have romanticized the rearing of Jesus, but we must remember that Mary and Joseph had some hard times. The tension came as Jesus began to figure out who he was and what he was supposed to do. He was torn between being a good son to Mary and Joseph and being the Messiah he was meant to embody. The more the Messiah assignment became clear in his mind, the more tension he must have undergone at home. But wait, you wonder, don't *all* kids have a hard time growing up? Absolutely! So, what exactly is the text telling us?

(1) At 12 Jesus began to have inklings of who he was and what he was supposed to do. This is not fantastic. At a Royal Ambassador camp, when I was 11 years old, I had my first clear impression

that I was "called" to be a preacher. I did not go public with it right away, and to be honest, I didn't think anyone would take me seriously. But regardless, I still remember. It was the first signal I received pointing me toward the path I would follow throughout the rest of my life. If I could think such profound thoughts at 11, what could Jesus the Messiah possibly have been thinking at 12? All too often, we underestimate our children, but when family and tradition reinforce each other, 12-year-olds often think ahead of us.

(2) "'Why were you searching for me? Did you not know that I must be in my Father's house?' But they did not understand what he said to them" (2:49-50). As Jesus was trying to figure out who he was and what God meant for him to do, Joseph and Mary were struggling themselves. Mary and Joseph wanted to be obedient to God's call for Jesus; they did not want to frustrate God or the maturing Jesus. Yet, at the same time, they simply couldn't leave a 12-year-old alone for an indefinite time in a big city. When a teenager wants to pull away, often it is not to a wayward lifestyle. The call to independence, identity, and vocation can collide with being an obedient son or daughter. Parents want to give freedom, and the maturing child wants to get along with their parents, but somehow all the pieces don't fit. But, while we're on the subject, don't you find it a bit comforting to know that Mary, Joseph, and Jesus had the same problems we do?

(3) "Then he went down with them and came to Nazareth, and was obedient to them. His mother treasured all these things in her heart" (2:51). Essentially, what this means is that Jesus went back home and became a 12-year-old again. "Luke saw the divine as coming not through the strange but through the familiar...God does not have to be identified with halos, but all the common facts of life are hallowed if the heavenly purpose is working there" (Walter Russell Bowie, *The Compassionate Christ*, New York: Abingdon Press, 1965, 58). A blessed child is not a "rich" child; a blessed child is one who has godly parents that take the time to actually parent. Joseph and Mary did their part, just as God knew they would. And, even though Jesus was becoming the "very Son of God," he was obedient to his parents. Should Jesus have stayed in Jerusalem when he had not told his parents

what he was doing? I don't know the answer to that one. Should children obey their parents as Jesus *usually* did? Now, for *that* one, I *do* know the answer.

A Son of God: Awareness and Identity, 2:49, 52.

At last, Mary and Joseph finally found Jesus. He was in the Temple, listening to teachers explain the law. Mary confronted him, "Child, why have you treated us like this?" (2:48b). Then came a provocative answer from the boy Jesus: "Why were you searching for me? Did you not know that I must be in my Father's house?" (2:49). All the commentators I've read on this text move in the same direction. All believe Jesus had some awareness of who he was and what he was supposed to do with his life. All, however, do not concur on the degree of awareness.

• According to Barclay, "...now comes one of the key passages in the life of Jesus. 'Your father and I,' said Mary, 'have been looking for you anxiously.' 'Did you not realize,' said Jesus, 'that you would find me in my Father's house?' See how very gently but definitely Jesus takes the name Father from Joseph and gives it to God...Here we have the story of the day when Jesus discovered who he was" (*The Gospel of Luke*, 24-5).
• Craddock, on the other hand, is not so sure: "Let us at this stage of Jesus' life simply say that there were in him vague stirrings of his own identity, if not vocation. The circle of his awareness and the sense of a larger duty begin to widen and deepen beyond the home in Nazareth" (*Luke*, Interpretation, 43).

I have to say that I perceive Barclay as a bit too confident in his ideas, while Fred Craddock's assertions are nearer my own understanding of what was happening in the mind of Jesus. But remember, *all* of us are guessing at best, taking our own experiences in coming to self-awareness (growing up), reading the text through the lens of our experience, and offering opinion. However, this much is clear: Mary understood all these things better when she looked back on them than she did in the moment. Martin Buber said, "No one walks with God, but sometimes we can track him." In the moment Mary did not understand what Jesus said to her in the Temple. But years later, she saw these same events in a much larger light. Jesus could not have known who he was when he was just a baby in the manger, but along the way, he had to grow gradually into the knowledge of God's will for his life.

It's important that we don't miss the points underlying this session. In our churches are earnest, intelligent youth. These are good kids who are trying to sort out, sift through, discover who they are and who they are meant to become. Granted, we may not take our young people to Jerusalem and Passover once a year, but we *do* take them to camps, to mission trips, to retreats. During these special events, they get clues, hints, voices suggesting to them the direction God is leading.

Our job is not easy. We can't tell youth "the will of God" for their lives. Anyway, we don't know the mind of God to speak for God in the first place. That's something young people have to figure out for themselves. But, we can be attentive, careful to watch and encourage. God is calling out leaders for the church in every generation. And, when one of our own is curious and lingers to learn more, take note. This lesson's Scripture is not point-blank history; it is sensitivity training for us all. The next generation of church leadership is in the balance.

Notes

Notes

Lesson 3 Study

May I Introduce You to a Friend?

Luke 3:15-22

Central Question

What are my expectations for Jesus?

Scripture

Luke 3:15-22 As the people were filled with expectation, and all were questioning in their hearts concerning John, whether he might be the Messiah, 16 John answered all of them by saying, "I baptize you with water; but one who is more powerful than I is coming; I am not worthy to untie the thong of his sandals. He will baptize you with the Holy Spirit and fire. 17 His winnowing fork is in his hand, to clear his threshing floor and to gather the wheat into his granary; but the chaff he will burn with unquenchable fire." 18 So, with many other exhortations, he proclaimed the good news to the people. 19 But Herod the ruler, who had been rebuked by him because of Herodias, his brother's wife, and because of all the evil things that Herod had done, 20 added to them all by shutting up John in prison. 21 Now when all the people were baptized, and when Jesus also had been baptized and was praying, the heaven was opened, 22 and the Holy Spirit descended upon him in bodily form like a dove. And a voice came from heaven, "You are my Son, the Beloved; with you I am well pleased."

Remembering

We left our story last lesson in Nazareth. Jesus was 12 years old, growing in wisdom and stature and also in divine as well as human favor. This lesson's story, however, picks up about 18 years later. The date is approximately AD 27, and true to form, Luke not only paints for us a cultural backdrop, but also provides us with all the so-called subtleties in the process—that is, names, names, and more names. When we enter the account, the country is under Roman rule. During this time, Tiberius, the successor of Augustus, was the second of the Roman emperors, and Pilate was the governor of Palestine. The religious authorities were Annas and Caiaphas. More specifically, although Caiaphas was the reigning high priest, Annas, whose term had technically ended in AD 14, remained the power behind the throne.

> Upon his death in 4 BC, Herod the Great, who was King of Judea during this era, divided his kingdom between three of his sons. Herod Antipas was appointed to rule Galilee and Peraea, and his reign lasted from 4 BC until AD 39. Herod Philip, on the other hand, was assigned to oversee Ituraea and Trachonitis from 4 BC to AD 33, during which time he built Caesarea Philippi, which obviously was named after him. Finally, Archelaus reigned over Judea, Samaria, and Edom, although the term "reigned" is used rather loosely. He was a terrible king. In fact, the Jews petitioned Rome and had Archelaus removed as king, after which Rome installed Pilate as the Roman procurator or governor from AD 25 until AD 37 (Barclay, 31).

It was against this backdrop that the Word of God came to John, son of Zechariah and Elizabeth, in the wilderness. John was well aware that his mission was to prepare the way for the Lord. Like a courier who went ahead of the king telling the people to prepare the roads prior to the king's visit, John's message called for the preparation of one's heart. To symbolize this metamorphosis of spirit, the prophet baptized with water, an outward illustration of an inward change.

> Once you entered [the water], you took off your garment, and this was an image of taking off the old person with its deeds. Having taken this off you were naked...You were naked in the sight of all and were not ashamed. For truly

you were bearing a copy of the first formed Adam, who in paradise was naked and not ashamed. (Cyril of Jerusalem)

Throngs of people gathered in the wilderness to hear John's message. Just imagine this awe-inspiring scene, if you will: Jews going out into the desert or wilderness, being baptized in the Jordan and then returning to the "Promised Land." It was a vivid reminder of God's delivering the Hebrew people out of Egypt and into the Promised Land. John's was a visual sermon that very well may have been intentionally so!

Unfortunately, some regarded John's baptism as a "magical rite which could make impenitent men safe in the hour of judgment" (Erdman, 41), yet this great prophet's baptism was far from magical. It was one of repentance. And according to John himself, repentance requires more than just a change of heart. In fact, John insisted that our daily lives act as a reflection of the change within us. He called for individuals to forsake their sins and then, in turn, to live accordingly.

In the few short verses of this Scripture, Luke illustrates two kinds of authority: First, Tiberius represents earthly authority with all its trappings and downfalls. John, on the other hand, represents heavenly authority, which seeks no recognition but continually points beyond one's self to God.

Studying

John the Messiah? (3:15) A prophetic word had not been heard since the days of Malachi. But with the words of John, four hundred years of silence had ceased. As was the case with the prophets who preceded him, John's message was one of sin and judgment, of repentance and pardon. Those who gathered in the wilderness to hear the prophet's message were filled with expectation. They wondered if this man could possibly be the Messiah, the chosen one they had been waiting for—the one who was to deliver them from their transgressions. Not surprisingly, the question took very little time to form in hopeful hearts: "Who is this man in the wilderness that takes us through the Jordan River to the Promised Land?"

John Introduces Jesus (3:16-18)
John assured the crowds that he was not the Messiah. In fact, he could not emphasize enough that Jesus' mission would be far greater than his own, for Jesus' power would be transforming. John preached that his baptism was significant, but nevertheless merely a ritual which symbolized an inward change, whereas Jesus would come to baptize with Spirit and fire. John's message called for change in one's life; Jesus' message called for a life carried out in relationship to God. John's words painted a picture of judgment, but Jesus' presence called for good and evil to be separated. Like chaff separated from the grain, evil would be removed and burned "with unquenchable fire."

> "I will sprinkle clean water upon you, and you shall be clean from all your uncleannesses, and from all your idols I will cleanse you." (Ezek 36:25)

John Is Imprisoned (3:19-20)
By no means was John's bold preaching confined to proclaiming the coming Messiah. John was all too aware of the immoral lifestyle of Herod Antipas, tetrarch of the region. Herod had married his brother's wife Herodias, who was not only Herod's sister-in-law, but also his niece. In addition, she was the daughter of yet another half-brother, Aristobulus. Herod's marriage was in blatant and irreverent opposition to Jewish law, and John purposely rebuked him for his lascivious behavior. As "reward" for what he saw as John's brazen criticism, Herod threw the prophet into prison. After all, no ruler would allow such rebuke from a mere "commoner."

> The winnowing fork, a flat wooden shovel, was used to separate the chaff from the grain. The grain was lifted off the floor by the winnowing fork and tossed high into the air. Even as the heavy grain would fall back to the floor, the chaff was blown away in the process (Barclay, 34).

Jesus Is Baptized (3:21-22) Portraying an image of direct contact with God, Luke tells us that "when Jesus also had been baptized and was praying, the heaven was opened, " at which point the Holy Spirit descended upon him like a dove. The baptism accounts in Matthew and Mark describe Jesus as coming up out of the water and the Holy Spirit descending upon him at that moment, empowering him for the journey that lay ahead. In Luke's Gospel, however, a voice from heaven says, "You are my Son, the Beloved; with you I am well pleased." We are not sure who heard these words of blessing and commission, but they were the final affirmation Jesus needed before beginning his earthly ministry.

> The dove was a symbol of "the beneficence of divinity in love, the loving character of divine life itself." The Holy Spirit descending on Jesus in the form of a dove would communicate to Mediterranean hearers that Jesus was beloved of God (Goodenough, 40-1).

That John's baptism was one of repentance begs the question, "Why, then, was Jesus baptized?" Some have speculated that he was baptized to affirm John's work and message. Others believe that Jesus was baptized in order to identify himself with his people. Still others are of the opinion that Jesus' baptism marked a transition point in his life. Just as anyone else who was baptized to symbolize the leaving of the old and laying hold to the new, so was Jesus also baptized in the same spirit, leaving years of preparation behind to begin years of ministry and service (Erdman, 43).

> "Water was used as a symbol of purification in many religions at a very early date. In the ancient world, the waters of the Ganges in India, the Euphrates in Babylonia, and the Nile in Egypt were used for sacred baths. The sacred bath was also known in Hellenistic mystery cults" ("Baptism," 1).

Understanding

Although expectations often can lead to disappointment, sometimes they lead to wonderful surprises. We have all experienced those delightful times in our lives when we expect one thing, only to be pleasantly taken off guard when what we get far exceeds our initial anticipations. In AD 27 the people of God had not heard a word from the Lord in four hundred years, and it would not be unrealistic to assume that after such a bewildering span of silence, expectations were not very high. Then suddenly a word from the Lord comes from John the Baptist—a word of sin and judgment, of repentance and pardon, but most importantly, of hope!

Because the Hebrews studied the Scriptures rigorously, they knew that John's message was filled with Messianic imagery: deliverance, repentance, and pardon. How could they go wrong to follow him? Because the prophet's message changed lives and attracted many followers, it is no wonder that some mistakenly deemed him the Messiah. However, when questioned outright, John points to another as the long-awaited Messiah, one that far exceeds anyone's expectations: Jesus, who will make things right, who will punish the evil and reward the good. Needless to say, John's introduction of Jesus heightened the expectations of all his listeners.

So, just what exactly are our expectations for Jesus? Redemption, of course, but anything else? If we answer in the negative, then we are no better than "the brood of vipers" that John calls some of his followers. Their only reason for baptism was to ensure their own redemption, but little did they realize that Jesus offered so much more. What if our expectations of Jesus directed us into a new life, one empowered by God's Spirit, lived in community with others and in relationship with God?

Plain and simple, our expectations of Jesus affect our introduction of him. In other words, if all Jesus provides is redemption, then our introduction of Jesus will be that of Savior. On the other hand, if all Jesus provides is companionship, our introduction of him will be that of Friend. Along these same lines, if all Jesus provides is healing, our introduction of him will be that of Physician. Then again, if all Jesus provides is teaching, then our introduction of him will be that of Rabbi. But blessing of all blessings, if Jesus has changed our lives, our very beings, our futures, then our introduction of Jesus will be that of Lord.

John introduced Jesus as Lord. In fact, John prepared the way for Jesus. Although Luke's account makes it seem as though John was imprisoned even before Jesus' baptism, other Gospels record that John continued his ministry, preaching the message of repentance and always pointing to Jesus. How easy it would have been for John to stay in the limelight! But, staying true to his righteous character, John understood the light of Jesus and wanted it to shine.

Like John, we are also called to introduce Jesus, always allowing Jesus to shine *through* us. In order for this to happen, we must neither get in the way of God's grace and love nor allow our prejudices to hinder the light of God. Besides, there is a great deal of truth in the old cliché that we might be the only "Jesus" that some folks ever know.

Jesus' baptism serves as an example for us all. It marked the end of *preparation* for ministry and the beginning of *doing* ministry. Jesus' baptism was a milestone, a turning point in his life, for it was at that point that he received the affirmation and blessing from God he needed to send him on his way. Likewise, our own baptism also is a symbol of a new life committed to God. And while it certainly is a sign of repentance, the fruits of our living are the true measure of that repentance. Anyone can enter the waters, but it takes grave commitment to walk in faith and allow Jesus to shine.

What About Me?

- *Describe the Jesus you know.* Take a few moments to examine your testimony of Jesus. What do you really know about him? Can you share accurately with others about Jesus' life and ministry on earth? How would you go about defining the difference Jesus has made in your life?

- *Examine your life.* Imagine that your life is portrayed by two light bulbs, one representing you and the other representing Jesus. Which bulb would be brighter? What changes can you make that would allow the light of Jesus to shine more completely through you?

- *Check the condition of your outward signs.* Baptism is an external sign of an internal change. What are some other outward signs that point to internal changes? What outward signs do you see in yourself?

- *Introduce Jesus to someone else.* John introduced Jesus to the world! Who introduced Jesus to you? To whom have you introduced Jesus? Never miss an opportunity to share with another person something new you have learned about Christ.

Resources

"Baptism," Microsoft® Encarta® Online Encyclopedia 2000 <http://encarta.msn.com> 1997-2000 Microsoft Corporation. All rights reserved.

William Barclay, *The Gospel of Luke* (Philadelphia: The Westminster Press, 1975).

Charles R. Erdman, *The Gospel of Luke* (Philadelphia: The Westminster Press, 1949).

S. MacLean Gilmour, "Luke," *The Interpreter's Bible*, vol. 8 (New York: Abingdon Press, 1952).

E. R. Goodenough, *Jewish Symbols in the Greco-Roman Period* (New York: Pantheon Books, 1953) 40-1.

Lesson 3   Commentary

May I Introduce You to a Friend?
Luke 3:15-22

Introduction

This lesson's text brings us to a turn in the road. Up to this point, Jesus has been just a promise—a very wonderful, exciting promise certainly, but a promise nonetheless. As you remember, our first session was solely about recognition. Even though people of unusual piety and faith could foresee what a little baby would become, the infant had not actually *done* anything—*yet*. Moving on to our second session, we were introduced to Jesus as a 12-year-old boy, precocious and insightful beyond his years. And yet, even at this time, he was still a boy, still a promise waiting to be fulfilled. In this session, however, we get to see the promise begin to take shape, as Jesus moves from quiet Nazareth—not to mention, sheer obscurity—to take center-stage before John the Baptizer as well as the numerous crowds who witnessed the onset of his public ministry.

Even though there are three distinct divisions in our passage, it is clear that the comment about Jesus' baptism (3:21-22) takes precedence over the other two sections regarding John the Baptist (3:15-17) and Herod Antipas, the man who put John in prison (3:18-20). Readers may be surprised to learn that even John the Baptist will not get full treatment, but this session is not about John the Baptist, but rather, about the role he played in introducing Jesus to the world.

A Saint Introduced Jesus, 3:15-17.

John the Baptist was a saint by any measure. In fact, in order to write this particular session, I had to venture outside our passage to collect ample research into John's character (see Lk 3:1-14;

Mt 3; Jn 1:19-37). As mentioned earlier, John may not be our main focus, but regardless, we need to know as much about him as we can to gain a thorough understanding of his person.

(1) By any standards, John was definitely "different." This son of Zechariah and Elizabeth ate unusual food, dressed in bizarre clothes, and made not so much as the slightest effort to court favor with either the religious establishment or the masses. He held his revival in the Judean wilderness, and to hear him people had to walk 40 miles into what we would call a desert. Obviously, John was not into "public relations."

(2) He was, however, into morality. Nobody left one of John's sermons wondering what point he was trying to make. When it came to right and wrong, he voiced his opinions plainly and directly. "And the crowds asked him, 'What shall we do?' In reply he said to them, 'Whoever has two coats must share with anyone who has none; and whoever has food must do likewise'" (3:10-11).

Walter Russell Bowie remarked on this lesson's Scripture, "There is everlasting danger that the plain matter of morality may drop out of preaching and drop out of people's idea of what religion is" (*The Compassionate Christ*, New York: Abingdon Press, 1965, 64). Bowie's right, as John reminds us. Grace trumps law, but grace does not negate right and wrong.

(3) John never forgot who he was and what he came to do. His preaching revived hope among "commoners," and in doing so, stirred wonder within their minds as to whether John actually could be *the* Messiah (see 3:15)! This was an obvious opening for John; after all, he easily could have taken his enormous popularity and turned it to private advantage. But there was nothing false about this man. "John answered all of them by saying, 'I baptize you with water; but one who is more powerful than I is coming; I am not worthy to untie the thong of his sandals'" (3:16). Interestingly enough, John is mentioned in each of the Gospels, all of which assign to him the mission of introducing Jesus. Without question, that is what John was born to do.

In the larger plot of the Bible, John the Baptist was a bit player. Besides, no one can deny that he was no Abraham or

Moses, Jesus or Paul. Yet, in his own time John the Baptist was assumed by many to be the Messiah, which clearly shows that he must have made a strong impression on a lot of people. John awakened people who were spiritually dead, elevating religion from little more than mere ritual to authentically decent, ethical living. But, most important of all, John paved the way for one much greater, willingly stepping into the background when it was time for Jesus to take his place on the very stage John had built. There is something pure, something appealing about a person who is willing not only to "play second fiddle," but also to play it well, without ever intending to steal away the spotlight from the soloist. Our churches could do nothing but benefit from a dose of John's grace.

A Villain Took John Away, 2:18-20.

"John was so plain and blunt a preacher of righteousness that he was bound to run into trouble" (William Barclay, *The Gospel of Luke*, Philadelphia: Westminster Press, 1956, 35). And, now that we mention it, he did. Herod the Great was the ruler when Jesus was born. After dying in 4 BC, his kingdom was divided among three of his sons. One of the sons, Herod Antipas, was given control over Galilee and Peraea, including the district where Jesus lived nearly all his life. To put it lightly, this Herod had the morals of an alley cat. In fact, once while on a visit to Rome, Herod Antipas seduced Herodias, his own half-brother's wife, into leaving her husband and moving to Palestine to marry him instead. It was this marriage that John the Baptist condemned so openly.

(1) John the Baptist did not just hint about the sins of Herod Antipas; he *nailed* them. And, Herod Antipas was not one to forgive and forget. In fact, Herod had a simple plan for getting John the Baptist to quiet down: he threw him into prison.
(2) It is apparent that Luke *really* wanted us to understand just how evil a man Herod Antipas was. Seducing his half-brother's wife was only one of his many sins! In biblical stories, it often seems as if the best people fall into the hands of the worst.

Jeremiah and Zedekiah, Jesus and Pilate, Paul and Nero—all prove my point.

(3) In short, we could say that Herod Antipas took John the Baptist "offstage." In other words, any potential rivalry that might have risen between John and Jesus had no opportunity to spark in the first place. John simply was not around. On the other hand, we do know that Jesus claimed a number of John's followers for his own (see Jn 1:37), and John's selfless attitude still commends him: "He must increase, but I must decrease" (Jn 3:30). Meanwhile, it is truly ironic that Herod Antipas made it into the history books at all. Had he never had a brush with Jesus, he probably would have just vanished, unremembered and forgotten. But since he did touch Jesus, even if only indirectly, we give him at least a nod.

A Savior Began His Ministry, 3:21-22.

"Now when all the people were baptized, and when Jesus also had been baptized and was praying..." (3:21a).

(1) The Setting

Jesus was baptized at a repentance revival. Repentance is not a whole gospel, but it is a start. Even though Jesus had no sins to forgive, still he wanted to support and bless all that John stood for. Besides, would it have made sense for Jesus to withhold himself from the best thing that was happening to the Jewish religion at the time? Our question about the necessity or appropriateness of Jesus' being baptized more than likely never even occurred to him.

You will also notice how often Luke surrounds the life of Jesus and the church in prayer. For instance, as Fred Craddock noted, Jesus was praying when the Holy Spirit came upon him, just as the church was praying when the Spirit came at Pentecost. Evidently, prayer was a pattern with Jesus and the early church, as it also ought to be a pattern with us (*Luke*, Interpretation, Louisville: John Knox Press, 1990, 52).

(2) The Baptism

• "Heaven was opened" (3:21b). Nothing was held back in equipping Jesus for service, for it is through Christ that God reaches out to us.

- "The Holy Spirit descended..." (3:22a). Does this mean the Spirit had not been with Jesus previously? I don't think so. Rather, I believe that an extra portion of the Spirit was poured out on Jesus for the work he was about to do. And this is constant with our own experience. During those times of special need, all of us have known what it feels like to receive an "extra helping" of the Spirit's power. This is how God has always cared for God's children, both then and now. Jesus, for example, would need the Spirit to fend off the Devil, to choose his disciples, to heal the sick, to speak parables, to get through Gethsemane and the Crucifixion—much more so than he did when he was a carpenter. When we have an immediate call to do God's work, we also can expect to be specially accompanied by the Holy Spirit.
- "A voice came from heaven, 'You are my Son, the Beloved; with you I am well pleased'" (3:22b). Whatever doubt may have remained in Jesus' mind about the work he had been sent to do had to be removed and replaced by the sense that he was on course. There is no indication that the "voice" from heaven was heard by others, but then again, it was meant for Jesus if for no one else.

Granted, when the topic turns to baptism, there are a number of directions we could take, but arguing about issues like whether immersion is better than sprinkling surely is *not* where this text takes us. Mainly, our passage reminds us to consider some key elements of our baptism experiences, including the question, does our baptism identify us with repentance? The baptism of Jesus did. Does our baptism define those times when we became Spirit-filled, Spirit-led individuals? Again, the baptism of Jesus did.

This session can be taught from the perspective of New Testament history, offering Jesus' story as a sort of sacred biography. But, if that is all we can make of it, that's a shame. God wants to bless us with the strength of the Spirit, and since Jesus received this empowerment at his own baptism, it seems hopeful that we might claim it as well.

Notes

Notes

Lesson  Study

Home is Where The Heart Is
Luke 4:14-30

Central Question

How do *you* respond to the message of Jesus?

Scripture

Luke 4:14-30 Then Jesus, filled with the power of the Spirit, returned to Galilee, and a report about him spread through all the surrounding country. 15 He began to teach in their synagogues and was praised by everyone. 16 When he came to Nazareth, where he had been brought up, he went to the synagogue on the sabbath day, as was his custom. He stood up to read, 17 and the scroll of the prophet Isaiah was given to him. He unrolled the scroll and found the place where it was written: 18 "The Spirit of the Lord is upon me, because he has anointed me to bring good news to the poor. He has sent me to proclaim release to the captives and recovery of sight to the blind, to let the oppressed go free, 19 to proclaim the year of the Lord's favor." 20 And he rolled up the scroll, gave it back to the attendant, and sat down. The eyes of all in the synagogue were fixed on him. 21 Then he began to say to them, "Today this scripture has been fulfilled in your hearing." 22 All spoke well of him and were amazed at the gracious words that came from his mouth. They said, "Is not this Joseph's son?" 23 He said to them, "Doubtless you will quote to me this proverb, 'Doctor, cure yourself!' And you will say, 'Do here also in your hometown the things that we have heard you did at Capernaum.'" 24 And he said, "Truly I tell you, no prophet is accepted in the prophet's hometown. 25 But the truth is, there were many widows in Israel in the time of Elijah, when the heaven was shut up three years and six months, and there was a severe famine over all the land; 26 yet Elijah was sent to none of them except to a widow at Zarephath in Sidon. 27 There were also many lepers in Israel in the time of the prophet Elisha, and none of them was cleansed except Naaman the Syrian." 28 When they heard this, all in the synagogue were filled with rage. 29 They got up, drove him out of the town, and led him to the brow of the hill on which their town was built, so that they might hurl him off the cliff. 30 But he passed through the midst of them and went on his way.

Remembering

We left our story last lesson at Jesus' baptism, when not only did the Holy Spirit descend upon him like a dove, but also a voice from heaven affirmed his title: Son of God. After this, the writer of Luke goes on to present the background details necessary to evidence that Jesus did indeed "fit the bill" of this esteemed title. In fact, the author divides the informative genealogy into three groups: first covering Adam to Abraham, then Abraham to David, and finally, David to Jesus.

By emphasizing the relationship of Jesus to David and Abraham, the writer of Luke clearly is targeting a Jewish audience. And unlike Matthew's, Luke's genealogy brings to light Jesus' priestly descent. Meanwhile, Luke also follows the genealogy of Mary, while Matthew concentrates on the genealogy of Joseph to spotlight Jesus' royal descent. It is also of particular interest to note that Luke's genealogy shows Jesus' connection to the entire human race—Jew and Gentile alike. As Luke makes obvious, Jesus begins his ministry fulfilling two roles: the Son of Man *and* the Son of God (Barclay, 40-1).

Following Jesus' baptism, the Spirit guided him into the wilderness, where the Devil tempted him unceasingly for 40 days. Jesus ate nothing during this time, so naturally, at the end of the 40 days he was extremely hungry. In his weakness, the Devil tempted him again, hoping to take advantage of Jesus' appetite. This particular temptation is reminiscent of the first human sin in Eden, when Adam and Eve doubted God's goodness by giving in to the tantalizing fruit of sin.

The Devil's other malicious attacks were directed at Jesus' ambition and success. Namely, in addition to promising Jesus all the kingdoms of the world—pushing without success to persuade Jesus to become skeptical of God's power—the Devil also took a shot at his opponent's intellect. But when Jesus could not even be coerced into jumping from the pinnacle of the Temple as a sign of his denouncement of God's wisdom, the Devil knew he had been beat. In fact, Jesus consistently responded to the Devil's advances with a word from God. Defeated but still determined, the Devil left him until a more "opportune time."

> "Luke's line of descent for Jesus runs through seventy-seven names to Adam and through him to God. The genealogy ends with the affirmation that Adam is the Son of God. This conditions the way one understands Jesus as Son of God in 4:3, 9. Just as Adam was Son of God, that is, a direct creation of God, so is Jesus Son of God, because he too is a direct creation of God (1:35). Read in this way the genealogy evokes the concept of Jesus as the second Adam" (Talbert, 46-7).

Studying

Jesus' Ministry in Galilee (4:14-15) It was after the wilderness excursion that Jesus began his ministry, and following this period in his life, we start to get deeper into Jesus' actual teaching. Filled with the power of the Spirit, Jesus returned to Galilee, about 80 miles north of Jerusalem and encircled by non-Jewish nations (it comes as no surprise, then, that the Hebrew word for circle is *Galil*). Galilee consisted of 204 villages and towns, all of which boasted on average about 15,000 residents each, residents who no doubt were especially drawn to the fertile land and wonderful climate of the region—not to mention the abundant water supply. It is no wonder that it earned the honor of being called the "garden of Palestine."

We are told that a report preceded Jesus' visit to Galilee, a report which spread quickly throughout the area. And naturally, we are left to wonder exactly what this report entailed. Did it consist of expectations the people had of Jesus? Or perhaps it consisted of speculations. "I wonder if he will continue working in his dad's carpenter shop." "I wonder if he'll stay in Nazareth." Then again, of course there is always the quite plausible chance that all the wild banter was about Jesus' legacy of miracles he had performed.

> The full name for Galilee is "Gelil ha-goyim," which means "district of the pagans." A Jewish king reunited the region with Judea, giving its people a generous choice between either circumcision or banishment. The Jewish faith took root in Galilee as Jewish families were transported into the area and given large tracts of land (de Vaux, 302).

While in Galilee, Jesus taught in the synagogue, restricted for the purpose of teaching and deemed the single most important building in the entire town. To illustrate, within each Galilean community that had a mere ten or more Jewish families, there was a synagogue. In fact, the synagogue was so revered that no sacrifices were allowed within its walls, only in the Temple.

> In its assembly room, men came to study and pray. In its courtyard, people would gather to discuss their family affairs or the village news. Marriages were celebrated in the synagogue, and the whole town turned out to gaze at the bride and to feast and dance. When a traveler needed shelter, he came to the synagogue. When a man needed food, he knew that the synagogue was the place to go. The little flat-roofed building was the center of village life. Day and night, its doors were kept open...The synagogue was the school where everyone was equal, where elders, farmers, priests, carpenters, weavers, merchants, could all come to study the laws of Moses and the teachings of the prophets. (Pessin, 45-6)

Jesus' Ministry in Nazareth (4:16-30) Next on the agenda, Jesus moved on to Nazareth, his hometown. Nazareth was a town in the hills of Galilee, full of crossroads, one of which led to Jerusalem. Many a pilgrim made their way through Nazareth on the way to Jerusalem for the Festival of Passover. Jews making this particular journey could find a haven in the synagogue there, where they could also pick up the news from surrounding towns and countries.

The passage for this lesson tells us that on the Sabbath Jesus went to the synagogue "as was his custom." The people of the Nazarene synagogue were fully aware of who Jesus was, and likewise, Jesus knew them. After all, he had grown up in that very synagogue, where he first learned of the laws of Moses and heard the words of the prophets.

On each Sabbath, the service at the synagogue consisted of three parts, the first being a time of worship. During this time, the Shema was recited and prayer was offered. The second part of the service involved the reading of the Scripture by seven members of the congregation selected to recite the chosen texts. Each of these readings consisted of a fixed lection from the Law and a free lection from the Prophets. The reading from the Law was predetermined to ensure that over a period of three years the entire Law was read. The reading from the Prophets, on the other hand, was determined each time by whoever had been chosen to read. Everyone read from a scroll in ancient Hebrew, while a translator (Targumist) interpreted the passage verse by verse into Aramaic. Also of interest, Scriptures from the Law were translated one verse at a time, while Scriptures from the Prophets were translated three at a time. The third part of the service entailed an explanation, along with an application of one or both of the Scripture passages offered. The service typically ended with a blessing by a priest or a prayer by a

> The Hebrew term "Shema"—the first word of the text—means, "hear": "'Hear, O Israel: The Lord is our God, the Lord alone.' You shall love the Lord your God with all your heart, and with all your soul, and with all your might. Keep these words that I am commanding you today in your heart. Recite them to your children and talk about them when you are at home and when you are away, when you lie down and when you rise. Bind them as a sign on your hand, fix them as an emblem on your forehead, and write them on the doorposts of your house and on your gates." (Deut 6:4-9)

> The Chazzan was an official in the synagogue, the cantor. Among his other duties—such as teaching, keeping the synagogue clean, and signaling the coming of the Sabbath each week with three blasts of the silver trumpet—the Chazzan also was responsible for taking out and putting back the sacred scrolls. In fact, it was he who handed Jesus the scroll of Isaiah (Barclay, 48).

layperson, and it was considered common practice to stand up to read and to sit down to preach.

Jesus was asked to read from the Prophets, so he was free to select the text he felt was appropriate. The passage he chose was from Isaiah. After reading the text before his listeners, Jesus sat down and made the application of the Isaiah material by saying, "Today, this Scripture has been fulfilled in your hearing." All seemed well at first. Those who had gathered spoke well of him and were amazed at his words. Come to think of it, the scene until this point should remind us of Jesus' first visit to the Temple. As you remember, when Mary and Joseph finally found him, they also discovered an attentive crowd of people who were amazed at Jesus' understanding and answers—which far exceeded his years. So, just what happens in the scene to drive a captivated audience into becoming a lynching mob?

It was as though Jesus heard the question from the audience: "Is not this Joseph's son?" His response indicated that there had been reports of his ministry, namely a desire that he "perform" in Nazareth. Yet, Jesus' use of a line from a papyrus fragment dated early third century AD really caused a stir: "No prophet is acceptable in his own country, and no physician performs cures on those who know him." However, he added to the proverb two stories from the Old Testament that speak favor of the Gentiles: that of the widow of Zarephath's hospitality to Elijah, as well as that of the healing of Naaman, the Syrian. As one would expect, the crowd was filled with rage, so much in fact that they chased him out of town to the brow of a hill, intending to throw him off. But Jesus stepped through the crowd and started making his way to Capernaum. We do not know if he ever visited Nazareth again.

Understanding

It is safe to assume that Jesus' experience in the wilderness was, at best, difficult; however, perhaps an even more trying moment for him was when he found himself preaching to the home crowd, the very same folks who had watched him grow up. After all, could there be a tougher audience, especially considering that the people from one's hometown always seem to have the hardest time overlooking the past?

The effect of Jesus' words in our passage was at least threefold. First, he was implying that the hometown crowd was seriously lacking people of faith. Unable to see beyond their familiarity with the "son of Joseph," the crowd could not focus on the presence—the workings—of God in the man they knew as Jesus. In effect, they could not see the trees for the forest. Their inability to discern God's work in Jesus limited their perspective. Maybe too often we look and listen only with our eyes and our ears, thereby missing the real presence of God among us.

Secondly, Jesus was insinuating that because these children of promise—children of Abraham—were not a people of faith, salvation would come to the Gentiles before many of them. Using Old Testament examples from the unfaithful days of ancient Israel, Jesus showed that God had indeed turned to Gentiles before and might very well do so again. At the bottom line, Jesus was offering a hard word of criticism against the lack of faithfulness among the people of his hometown.

Finally, the prophecy from Isaiah that Jesus read in the synagogue that day declared Jesus' mission and purpose. The Spirit of the Lord was upon him, and in fact, it was through the Spirit that his ministry began, his ministry to bring "good news to the poor…to proclaim release to the captives and recovery of sight to the blind…to let the oppressed go free…and proclaim the year of the Lord's favor."

We are never told that the service was concluded after Jesus' interpretation of the Isaiah text, but we do know that the crowd drove him out of the synagogue. Did the service continue through the blessing and the prayer, or was it so "tainted" with Jesus' comments that no one could bear to go on? How appropriate if the service that day *had* been left incomplete, for after all, Jesus' ministry *still* continues today—within the life of the church and within each individual. Keep in mind, though, that the Isaiah text has yet to be fully lived out. Maybe the blessing and prayer from that initial service in Nazareth are yet to come!

What About Me?

- *Examine your faith walk.* What is your purpose? How does your mission in life measure up to that of Jesus? How can you better align your own mission and purpose with that of Christ? And on a broader scale, how can the church better align its mission and purpose with that of Jesus?

- *Examine your response to Jesus.* When Jesus calls on you to respond to his Word, to his mission, to his purpose, how do you answer? Have you helped Jesus feel "at home" in your heart, or is he merely visiting? When you hear something new about Jesus, how do you respond: with disbelief or with gratitude, thanking God for opening your eyes and your mind to a clearer picture of God's Son?

- *Examine your commitment to God.* How easy it is for us to "buck up" against words of critique, especially when those words concern our spirituality! Too easily we make our spiritual lives yet another competition, another climb up the ladder. What would happen if we allowed ourselves to be open to the honest, insightful, and loving care of our spiritual brothers and sisters? To do this, would it not require that we commit ourselves to God in a very deep and relational manner?

Resources

William Barclay, *The Gospel of Luke* (Philadelphia: The Westminster Press, 1975).

Roland de Vaux, "The World of Jesus," *Everyday Life in Bible Times* (Washington DC: National Geographic Society, 1967).

Charles R. Erdman, *The Gospel of Luke* (Philadelphia: The Westminster Press, 1949).

Rev. Joseph M. Gettys, Ph.D., *How to Study Luke* (Richmond: John Knox Press, 1947).

S. MacLean Gilmour, "Luke," *The Interpreter's Bible*, vol. 8 (New York: Abingdon Press, 1952).

E. R. Goodenough, *Jewish Symbols in the Greco-Roman Period* (New York: Pantheon Books, 1953) 40-1.

HOME IS WHERE THE HEART IS

Luke 4:14-30

Introduction

In a sad way, this lesson's Scripture text supplies an appropriate ending for a series titled "Roots in Tradition and Family." Jesus had lived nearly all his life in the small town of Nazareth. It's probably a safe bet that the culture there resembled that of small towns today, where the same people have lived together for generations. In that kind of community, you need to be careful. Everybody is kin to everybody else. In fact, more than likely the synagogue that is the setting for our passage was the same one Jesus had attended all his life. No doubt about it, it was "Roots in Tradition and Family" with a flare. The hometown boy was back, and he had made quite a reputation for himself while he had been away. "A report about him spread through all the surrounding country" (Lk 4:14b). You can be sure the synagogue was packed that Saturday, standing room only, and somewhere in the crowd were Jesus' mother and siblings. Sure enough, Jesus had come home. They knew him, and likewise, he knew them.

Going back home is never easy. I remember well the few occasions I preached at my home church in Fort Worth. I always got especially nervous for those sermons, perhaps because the people there knew me in a way that I feared could cut through any education or reputation I had acquired as a preacher. As far as they were concerned, I was just plain ol' Cecil. Some of that same nervousness must have been present when Jesus was asked to take center-stage in the Nazareth synagogue. However, Luke does not unpack for us "how Jesus felt" about going back home. On the contrary, he was interested in more substantive issues, namely providing a sort of road map for the ministry of Jesus, a road map explaining who Jesus was and is, including what his message would be and how Jews in Nazareth, Jerusalem, and beyond would respond to it. In this particular case, we learn that Jesus was greeted with a favorable reception when he arrived in the Gentile community.

Pattern and Reputation, 4:14-17.

Most of us think of Jesus as a wanderer, an itinerant. Luke, however, wants us to change our way of thinking, insisting that Jesus actually followed a very calculated design in going about the work of the Kingdom:

(1) He began in Galilee. "Then Jesus...returned to Galilee" (4:14a). After his baptism/temptations, he went back to the people and the land that had been home, the people and the land that he knew best.

(2) He moved by the leading and "power of the Spirit" (4:14a). At baptism "the Holy Spirit descended upon him in bodily form" (3:22). Then "Jesus, full of the Holy Spirit, was led by the Spirit into the Wilderness, where...he was tempted" (4:1). Our text for this lesson opens with similar words: "Then Jesus, filled with the power of the Spirit, returned to Galilee..." (4:14). It may seem as though talk about the Holy Spirit has been diminished in many denominations today, but like Jesus, the apostles, and the saints, we as Christians all have access to the Spirit.

(3) He "began to teach in their synagogues" (4:15a). Jesus' pattern was to go to a synagogue, teach as a guest rabbi, and use the opportunity to explain the Old Testament. Unlike the Temple in Jerusalem, which was priest-led, the synagogue was a lay-led institution. Also, for the record, there were no synagogues until the Jews were taken captive by the Babylonians. When they could no longer go to Temple for worship, they created synagogues. Anywhere there were 10 heads of houses, there could be a synagogue. The services were comprised of everything from prayer and praise, to receiving instruction in the law and making offerings to the poor (Walter Russell Bowie, *The Interpreter's Bible*, vol. 8, New York: Abingdon Press, 1952, 89). Any layman or guest

rabbi could be asked to read from and make comment about the Old Testament.

Often we point out Jesus' condemnation of Judaism, but it is important to know that he began his ministry in the synagogues. Jesus was Jewish through and through. For all that is wrong with our modern churches, I believe that if Jesus were among us today, that is where he would start once again. Jesus went to church and we would be wise to follow his example.

(4) Jesus developed a reputation early on. "A report about him spread through all the surrounding country...He was praised by everyone" (4:14b-15). Evidently, Jesus' previous efforts toward public ministry which preceded his return home were well-received, and therefore, went before him. But, as we soon realize, everything changed once he actually "came to Nazareth" (4:16a).

Revelation and Proclamation, 4:18-21.

When mingling with the hometown crowd, Jesus was very firm both in communicating who he was and in refining his definition of the gospel.

(1) Revelation
The leader of the synagogue honored Jesus by asking him to read. He chose to read Isaiah 61:1-2, a "servant song" that looked forward to a coming Messiah who would relieve the oppression of God's people: "The Spirit of the Lord is upon me, because he has anointed me to bring good news to the poor...." "Then he began to say to them, 'Today this scripture has been fulfilled in your hearing'" (4:18, 21). In other words, Jesus was telling them straight out, "I am the Messiah; all the scriptures promised is fulfilled in your presence today." Fred Craddock adds, "'Anointed me' means 'made me the Christ or Messiah'" (62).

(2) Proclamation
The Messiah had come "to bring good news to the poor...to proclaim release to the captives and recovery of sight to the blind, to let the oppressed go free, to proclaim the year of the Lord's favor" (4:18b-19).

- "Good news to the poor." The gospel of Jesus has always targeted and been welcomed by "the poor." When Paul wrote to the quarreling Corinthians, he said, "Consider your own call, brothers and sisters: not many of you were wise by human standards, not many were powerful, not many were of noble birth" (1 Cor 1:26). It was the poor who were receptive to the gospel. Always the lively side of the church is the underside.

• Did Jesus mean to empty jails "to let the oppressed go free"? I don't think so. But, Jesus was saying that his gospel would touch real people from the real world. His was a gospel with an edge of justice. When people are abused, the gospel is aimed toward their relief. Where there is unfairness, the gospel works to make wrongs right. While we may do our best to make the gospel antiseptic, abstract, theoretical, Jesus made it a gospel that feels pain and brings relief to all who are suffering. In fact, this same theme pervades the African American spirituals that have come to be so beloved by many cultures.

• To "proclaim the year of the Lord's favor" means that the Kingdom of God is *now*, not far away in some remote, distant time: "The time is fulfilled, and the kingdom of God has come near; repent, and believe in the good news" (Mk 1:15). The Messiah is not "in the sweet by and by." The gospel is present tense.

Expectatoin and Hostility, 4:22-24.

"All spoke well of him and were amazed at his gracious words" (4:22). Then, almost immediately the same people became suspicious: "Is not this Joseph's son?" (4:22b). Jesus confirmed his awareness of the crowd's skepticism by saying, "Truly I tell you, no prophet is accepted in the prophet's hometown" (4:24). What are we to make of this? First they "spoke well of him," and then they cut him down.

Walter Russell Bowie offers a helpful suggestion: "It seems that in this passage Luke is combining material which had come to him from two different sources, so that the whole picture as he presents it is not quite consistent" (93). If we refer back to Mark, which was surely one of Luke's sources, we get a clearer picture. There is no question that the crowd was unfriendly from the start.

- They wanted Jesus to perform a miracle for them as he had done for people in other places. Yet, "...he could do no deed of power there, except that he laid his hands on a few sick people and cured them. And he was amazed at their unbelief" (Mk 6:5-6). It would suffice to say that their unbelief stifled the miraculous.
- They simply would not allow him to be the Messiah. That is, they would not grant him authority or wisdom. "Is not this Joseph's son?" (4:22b). When we know someone well, isn't it usually our tendency to remove from them the power to correct us, even if what they have to say is exactly the right thing? The old proverb "Familiarity breeds contempt" seems quite suitable for describing the people in the Nazareth synagogue. Had Jesus been a foreigner to their land, they might have granted him place and authority.

This incident fell early within the ministry of Jesus, but it was preview for what was to come. After all, how many times would the Jews show a special hostility toward Jesus? Often they picked at him or even tried to embarrass him by asking questions that they were sure would "show him up." Ultimately, they even would ask for his very life, choosing to release the criminal Barabbas rather than let Jesus live. "He came to what was his own, and his own people did not accept him" (Jn 1:11).

Offense and Departure, 4:25-30.

Admittedly, Jesus was greeted by suspicion before he had even opened his mouth, but he also did something that really offended his audience. Specifically, when they began to doubt him, he reached back into the Old Testament and came forward with two illustrations. Both put Gentiles in a good light, an unforgivable sin in the eyes of Jesus' Jewish audience.

- There was a great drought in Israel. The prophet Elijah "was sent...to Zarephath in Sidon" (4:26). This was outside Israel. He received his food and shelter from a Gentile woman. That there could be kindness and that God's prophet should have a care for

Gentiles was an unwelcome reminder. Jesus was stretching the boundaries.
• "There were also many lepers in Israel during the time of the prophet Elisha, and none of them was cleansed except Naaman, the Syrian" (4:27). The Nazareth audience got the point, and they resented both the message and the messenger.

And then, the sermon was over. In fact, it is highly unlikely that the service was ever officially finished, for "[w]hen they heard this, all in the synagogue were filled with rage. They got up, drove him out of the town..." (4:28-29a). Luke tells us that the crowd intended to kill Jesus by pushing him "off the cliff" that was near Nazareth, but it was not to be. "He passed through the midst of them and went on his way" (4:30). And it was over. Jesus had come home. The people wanted him to perform, but they were skeptical. When Jesus tried to tell them who he really was, what his gospel meant, who could be included in God's Kingdom, the people were offended to the point of rage.

The Jewish tradition that had nurtured a lively faith in him had come from Nazareth, yet his hometown smothered him with doubt, eventually running him out of town. And so, "Roots in Tradition and Family" ends with rejection. Jesus left Nazareth, and there is no record that he ever went back again.

Notes

Notes

www.ingramcontent.com/pod-product-compliance
Lightning Source LLC
Chambersburg PA
CBHW060705030426
42337CB00017B/2770